UNTANGLING JESUS FROM RELIGION

UNTANGLING JESUS FROM RELIGION

Marco DeBarros

XULON PRESS ELITE

Xulon Press Elite
2301 Lucien Way #415
Maitland, FL 32751
407.339.4217
www.xulonpress.com

Unless otherwise indicated, Scripture quotations taken from the Holy Bible, New Living Translation (NLT). Copyright ©1996, 2004, 2007 by Tyndale House Foundation. Used by permission of Tyndale House Publishers, Inc.

Scripture quotations taken from The Message (MSG). Copyright © 1993, 1994, 1995, 1996, 2000, 2001, 2002. Used by permission of NavPress Publishing Group. Used by permission. All rights reserved.

Printed in the United States of America.

Paperback ISBN-13: 978-1-66280-659-9
eBook ISBN-13: 978-1-6628-0660-5

DEDICATION

To my kids. I pray you are able to untangle all of the obstacles that gets in the way of Jesus sooner than later, so you may be able to fully enjoy this journey called life.

And to my wife Lindsey, you are the greatest gift that Jesus gave me.

TABLE OF CONTENTS

INTRODUCTION

UNTANGLING JESUS FROM RELIGION

THERE ARE ABOUT 4,300 religions in the world. I googled it.

Religion is the attempt to connect with the divine. It is the longing to make sense of life, meaning, and existence.

In a way, I think every single human being is religious, even those who claim no religion.

Everyone has a set of beliefs.

Everyone is trying to make sense of life.

Everyone is searching for meaning and purpose.

Everyone wonders if there's something out there other than what they see with their natural eyes.

Meaning, purpose, love, identity...these are all universal longings.

I don't think Jesus meant to start a religion in His name.

When I read the gospels, which are the main documents that tell us about Jesus, I don't see a desire for a religious movement, but more of a quest to bring meaning and purpose to humanity.

For example, in the gospel of John, Jesus said "My purpose is to give them a **rich** and **satisfying** life." (John 10:10)

That does not sound like someone who came to establish a set of belief systems, but more like someone who wanted to help people find true meaning for life.

As you read Jesus' encounters with different people, you get the sense that there was something very different about His approach and His heart for humanity.

Most were pleasantly surprised by his heart for them.

Jesus valued people, not religious standards.

Jesus made religious people uncomfortable, because He read through the emptiness of their empty rituals.

Jesus poked holes in value systems that kept people oppressed.

Jesus gave hope to the hopeless.

Jesus gave identity to the outcasts.

If we can untangle Jesus from religion, I think we will be pleasantly surprised.

I invite you to go on this journey with me, to discover the Jesus who came to give us a rich and satisfying life.

CHAPTER 1

MESS(AGE)

HAVE YOU EVER been overwhelmed by a mess?

We have five young kids, therefore, mess is just the norm in our house.

My wife, Lindsey, can't stand a messy house. Me on the other hand...well, I think I've become immune to it.

My favorite part of our house is the basement. It's the man cave. Actually, is the mess cave. It's where the kids keep all of their toys and are allowed to run wild and make all the mess possible. It is for most part out of sight from mom. My wife Lindsey does not like the basement. It is overwhelming for her to see such a mess.

I think that's how most people feel about religion. It's messy. With so many of them, how can you possibly know which one is true?

And good luck having a conversation about religion without it turning into a fight, leaving you even more frustrated.

So most people avoid it altogether. We say don't bring up religion and politics.

This is why I'm passionate about untangling Jesus from just mere religious talk.

What Jesus talks about is the longing of every human soul for meaning, purpose and identity.

It would be a shame to not untangle the mess to get to the message.

We are desperate for the very things that Jesus came to bring us.

Every few weeks, we tackle the basement mess. And each time, I'm so glad that we did, and it makes my wife very happy. You know the saying, happy wife, happy man cave, or something like that.

If we are willing to untangle Jesus from the mess of religion, I think our souls will be extremely glad.

Underneath the mess, there's a powerful message.

CHAPTER 2

JESUS VERSUS RELIGION

""**ARE YOU TIRED?** Worn out? Burned out on religion? Come to me. Get away with me and you'll recover your life. I'll show you how to take a real rest. Walk with me and work with me—watch how I do it. Learn the unforced rhythms of grace. I won't lay anything heavy or ill-fitting on you. Keep company with me and you'll learn to live freely and lightly."" - *Jesus (Matthew 11:28-30)*

These words from Jesus convince me that His goal was not to start a religion in His name.

Jesus came to earth as a Jewish man and his life was steeped in its culture and way of life. The

Jewish people believe that they are God's chosen and live by God's Word and will for their lives.

Keep in mind that the Jewish people had been waiting for the promised Messiah for many centuries and at this point in history, they were under the rule of the ruthless Roman Empire.

Jesus insisted that he came to fulfill the words of God to his people. He insisted that he was the embodiment of God's Word. He moved into the neighborhood to show us what it actually looked like to live in harmony with God and people.

As Jesus walked the earth, He sees that religion was actually doing the opposite of what it was intended.

Jesus could see and sense that people were tired and worn out, not just physically, but also emotionally and spiritually.

Religion without the heart of God will sap the life out of us. For those of us who grew up in religious settings, you know what I'm talking about. The religious demands can begin to weigh on your soul.

Religious routines can become detrimental to the soul. We feel obligated to do certain things, and then do them out of guilt and duty, not out of devotion and love. We are constantly working to appease our God, and get frustrated that we aren't producing the right fruits. There's no sense of excitement and truth be told, we are bored with the routine and lack of creativity or imagination. We feel ourselves living a defensive life, and not even sure of the why behind it all.

Religion can become impersonal.

We do it because we have to. We don't enjoy it. It feels more like taking medicine or eating your vegetables and trying to convince ourselves that it's the right thing to do. But there's no life in it. We try to keep up appearances but there's no power coming from it.

Religion gives us beliefs, but it does not always lead to convictions.

It's more of a private thing that we do on the weekends. We do it to earn God's approval. It's almost like a checklist:

Say your prayers, check.

Get confirmed, check.

Get baptized, check.

Try to be a nice person, check.

Go to church when you can, check.

And remember that God helps those who help themselves, check.

In the meantime, life is being sucked out of you.

The bottom line is that the religious routine is not having much of a positive effect on your life.

Jesus said, come to me, not to a religion. That's a personal invitation.

He said, walk with me and work with me. That's a partnership.

He also said, watch how I do it. That's a mentor or role model.

And my favorite part of his appeal is when he said, learn the unforced rhythms of grace.

Wait, life has a rhythm?

Jesus seems to be inviting us to a dance.

What is the soundtrack of your life? Or what's playing in your mind right now?

If it's not grace, then it's works.

If it's not peace, then it's chaos.

If it's not love, then it's self-hate.

Jesus is inviting to a dance, and he wants to lead the way.

In Jesus' days, farming was one of the major industries. In order to work the fields, they would use animals to help plow the land. Usually two cows would be yoked together to plow and thresh grain. Farmers would pair an experience cow with a younger less experienced one. The older and more experienced would lead the way. That way, working together they would yield the best results.

Jesus said, I won't lay anything heavy or ill-fitting on you. That's the image of the two animals being yoked together. He wants to lead us on this journey of life. Side by side. If he leads, we will yield much better results. Jesus is the more experienced one, so the pressure will be off of us.

Jesus said, keep company with me. In other words, let's do life together. This does not sound like a weekend thing, but more like a lifestyle.

The outcome is that you will live freely and lightly. That's Jesus' invitation to us.

I think that life is better with Jesus.

And I think that we are better at life because of Jesus.

But that only happens when we embrace his invitation to a relationship with him, and not just check a religious box.

Jesus says, come follow me.

The more you spend time with someone the more you get to know them and eventually trust them. That's what Jesus did with his first students. He invited them to follow him and they did for about 3 years. They were together 24/7 for those 3 years or so. These students, or apprentices, were to learn and do what Jesus does. Actually, Jesus calls them to follow him with the intention that they will do what he does, not just to watch him do it.

Those first students are just like us.

Just regular everyday people.

So, we can follow Jesus just as we are.

As they followed him and as we follow him, we learn that the invitation is for an eternal journey.

We don't need to earn his love or approval.

His invitation is saying that you are loved and approved.

I come just as I am.

Jesus is not grading our performance.

This is a grace invitation, not based on our works.

Jesus justifies me.

Jesus is my righteousness.

Jesus gives me new desires.

> "God saved you by his grace when
> you believed. And you can't take
> credit for this; it is a gift from God.
> Salvation is not a reward for the
> good things we have done, so none
> of us can boast about it. For we are
> God's masterpiece. He has created
> us anew in Christ Jesus, so we can
> do the good things he planned for
> us long ago."- ***Ephesians 2:8-10***

You know you are following Jesus, when your heart is responding out of love and not obligation. When you're dancing because you want to dance, not because you have to dance.

Duty is replaced with devotion.

"Have to" is replaced with wanting to.

Boredom is replaced with excitement.

Works are replaced with grace.

But there's a cost.

To follow Jesus, I must let go of my pride. In other words, I must let go of the illusion that I can lead myself.

I must let go of pretending. I don't have it all figured out and only God is truly good.

I must yield myself to Him. His grace is not forced. Jesus can't make me dance if I don't want to. In a dance, someone needs to lead or it's a train wreck.

So who's leading your life?

Are you tired?

Worn out?

Go to Jesus.

He's one prayer away.

Jesus, I want to recover my life. Teach me the unforced rhythms of grace. Amen.

CHAPTER 3

JESUS VERSUS LEGALISM

ONE TIME, JESUS and his students were hungry. They were walking through a grain field, and decided to break some heads of grain to eat.

No big deal, right?

Well, some Pharisees called them out on their spontaneous snacking. Why? They did it on the Sabbath.

According to the Pharisees, who were one of the main Jewish religious denominations of that time, they broke the law. More specific they broke the sabbath law (see Mark 2). To which you might say...this is why I don't bother with religion. It's pointless. Why are they upset of about some hungry people having a snack?

Let's untangle this.

The Pharisees like any other religious denominations meant well by their approach.

They did their best to interpret the Old Testament, which are the books of the Bible before Jesus.

They interpreted the laws and tried to make it relevant to their time period. They were very strict and believed it was how they showed their devotion to God.

You know the Ten Commandments right?

Go ahead and tell me what they are. Without cheating. Go.

Ok, let me help you. In the book of Exodus, God gave the Israelites the Ten Commandments. The Israelites had been oppressed by the Egyptians for over 400 years up to this point. Exodus tells us the account of how God had liberated them from a life of slavery to the Egyptians. The Ten Commandments was God's way of teaching them how to be free and live with a new sense of identity, meaning and purpose.

Much like those who have been incarcerated for long periods of time have difficulty adjusting to freedom, so did the Israelites. But, God in His goodness and likeness gave them these Ten Commandments (or principles) to live by.

Here they are:

1. There are no other gods, but only one God
2. Don't make idols, just worship the one true God
3. Don't take God's name in vain
4. Keep the Sabbath, meaning remember that God provides for you.
5. Honor your parents (all the parents said, AMEN)
6. Don't kill people

7. Don't commit adultery
8. Don't steal
9. Don't bear false witness against your neighbor
10. Don't covet other people's lives, families, and belongings (see Exodus 20).

Pretty good principles to live by. Don't you think?

Again, if you were a slave and didn't have a sense of identity and purpose, you would want to have principles to help you navigate through life.

If you pay close attention to these principles, they were meant to teach them how to love God and love people well.

The first four principles are about loving God properly and the next six are how to properly love your neighbor.

Over time, religious leaders felt compelled to help impose these principles, so they can live life according to God's will.

As time progressed, they kept adding to the commandments in order to keep up with the changes in culture and human behavior. By the time Jesus comes on the scene the religious laws and regulations had ballooned to many sub-laws. Good luck untangling that!

In its purest form, the law is good. Keeping the Sabbath is a good thing. We are so restless and driven by works, that God has to command us to rest. The goal was and is to rest and appreciate where all your blessings come from. But, does it mean that you can't enjoy a snack on a Sabbath, because it looks like you're working by picking out grain?

The Pharisees prided themselves on keeping the law and being completely set apart from the pagan culture of their day. They created a bunch of sub-laws with the intention of helping people in doing God's will.

Sometimes, the very thing that we think is keeping us from sinning, actually leads us to sin.

Sin means missing the point or missing the mark. In other words, religious laws can actually work against us when taken out of context.

So what does Jesus do?

He does what he does best. Jesus tells them a story.

Jesus tells them the story of a man in their Bible that they would be familiar with. Actually, one of their heroes, a man named David. A man that the Bible says was a man after God's heart (see Mark 2).

One time, David and his boys were hungry, so they went into the temple and broke the law by eating the sacred loaves of bread that only priests are allowed to eat.

That is equivalent to someone being hungry today and breaking into a church and eating the communion wafers.

> "Then Jesus said to them, "The Sabbath was made to meet the needs of people, and not people to meet the requirements of the Sabbath." - **Mark 2:27**

Say it again for the people in the back, Jesus.

The Sabbath or God's commandments were given to meet the needs of the people, and not people to meet the requirements of the Sabbath.

This is a powerful moment of untangling Jesus from religion.

Every commandment or principle has a heartbeat attached to it. And if it does not bring life to people, then it's just legalism or dead religion.

Legalism is the excessive adherence to law or formula.

God even tells us through his prophet Isaiah that you can do something external that looks right, but your heart may not be in it:

> "And so the Lord says, "These people say they are mine. They honor me with their lips, but their hearts are far from me. And their worship of me is nothing but man-made rules learned by rote." - ***Isaiah 29:13***

I remember growing up going to Catholic mass, and many people would be physically there, but not very interested in the mass. It was more like a religious routine than a meaningful experience with a living God.

Jesus goes on to say:

> "But you would not have condemned my innocent disciples if you knew the meaning of this Scripture: 'I want you to show mercy, not offer sacrifices.'" - ***Matthew 12:7***

The point of the commandments was always relationship. How to relate to God and how to relate to people.

If a commandment or religious practice is not compelling you to love God and people better, then it is no longer relevant, but legalistic.

Paul, another Bible writer tells us that the law was only meant to be a tutor until we mature in our understanding of God's grace:

> "Before the way of faith in Christ was available to us, we were placed under guard by the law. We were kept in protective custody, so to speak, until the way of faith was revealed. Let me put it another way. The law was our guardian until Christ came; it protected us until we could be made right with God through faith. And now that the way of faith has come, we no longer need the law as our guardian. For you are

> all children of God through faith
> in Christ Jesus. And all who have
> been united with Christ in baptism
> have put on Christ, like putting on
> new clothes." - ***Galatians 3:23-27***

Jesus is Lord, or boss, over the Sabbath and law.

We live by the grace of Jesus. We don't earn it, nor do we deserve it. There's nothing we can do to make Jesus love us more or less.

We live by His grace, not by keeping the law.

We don't behave to be accepted by God. Because we are accepted by God, we behave.

Love is what compels us to want to obey the commandments, because they were given to us by a loving God.

But, even by our utmost desire to obey all the commandments, we still fall short.

And that's where Jesus differs from religion.

Religion says you have to keep all the laws, rituals, regulations and jump through different hoops so that God can accept you.

Jesus says, I come to give my life as a perfect sacrifice so that you and I can be accepted, loved, and justified.

Jesus comes to satisfy a deeper hunger that we all have. Hunger for forgiveness, acceptance, meaning, purpose and identity.

So, go ahead and have a snack on the Sabbath! Better yet eat from the bread of life and you will never go hungry again.

CHAPTER 4

JESUS VERSUS TRADITIONS

> These people honor me with their
> lips, but their hearts are far from me
> - *Isaiah 29:13*

WHY ARE WE doing this?

What's the point?

Ever find yourself asking those questions? I think we all have. Some of us do it quietly and others are pretty blatant about it.

I was born and raised in the Cape Verde Islands. It's an archipelago of ten islands and I was fortunate to be from the best island and capital called

Santiago. Being colonized by the Portuguese, our country is highly influenced by the Catholic faith. Most people believe in God and go to church, at least for Easter and Christmas.

My parents were the Easter and Christmas church goers. I went every week, because of my grandmother. She was a devout Christian, and I believe the spiritual bedrock of our family. She made sure I went to Sunday school every single week.

My grandmother had two sisters. They were devout Catholics. And my grandmother went to a Nazarene church. They loved each other and never allowed their differences in denominations affect their relationship. Deep down, I think they knew that it was all about Jesus and not religion.

At some point, when I was about twelve years old, my aunts decided that I should also go to Catholic mass with them. I think that my aunts and my grandmother had a secret meeting about me. They decided that they will make sure I get to Jesus. On Sundays, I would go to Sunday school with my grandmother at the Nazarene church and Catholic mass at night with my aunts. So growing up, my denomination was Catherene (Catholic + Nazarene).

For Christmas, in Cape Verde, we would go to church at night on Christmas Eve. As a kid, I was always a part of the Christmas program. Singing, being in a play, or reciting verses and poems. After church, we would go back home and wait for midnight to open our gifts. I remember feeling so restless between the church service and midnight to open gifts.

In 1993, my parents and my two sisters moved to the United States. I was 15 years old. Somehow, my grandmother made a connection with a family in the States, to make sure I went to church weekly. Shout-out to the Pina family for picking me up for church every Sunday. At this point, my parents were still doing the Easter & Christmas church routine. And kept our opening gifts at midnight tradition.

Fast forward to a few years later, I got married and my wife and I started having kids right away. We have five of them (pray for us). My sisters also got married and had kids of their own. Even though we all moved, we continue to get together at my parents on Christmas Eve to continue our Christmas tradition of opening gifts at midnight.

We live in New England, and it's usually very cold in December. Getting five kids in a car during winter is a serious undertaking. It is a lot of work. Taking them to church and then getting them to wait until midnight to open gifts is the equivalent of day in purgatory. Not fun for them and not fun for us as parents.

So, one December, we asked the ultimate question, why are we doing this? Why are we torturing ourselves and our kids for the sake of an old tradition? We decided that it was time for a family meeting. Everyone agreed that it was foolish to continue that tradition of waiting until midnight to open the gifts. We all agreed to get together earlier in the day on Christmas Eve and allow the kids and ourselves to actually enjoy the day. Thank God!

One time, Jesus and his disciples were invited to a meal with some Pharisees and other religious leaders.

Jesus' disciples began eating without washing their hands. Which is kind of gross. But, this was not your typical washing of hands before you eat. The religious tradition of hand washing was for the purpose of spiritual cleansing. The Orthodox Jews of that time believed in being set apart from the rest of the world. So after going out in public and mingling with Gentiles, they felt the need to purify themselves from the world. Therefore, they took offense to the fact that Jesus' disciples were not purging themselves from the rest of the world by not participating in the hand washing ritual.

Jesus calls out their tradition as a substitute for the real thing. He calls it an empty ritual with no inner transformation. Man-made ideas that does not lead to inner transformation. Jesus makes his point by quoting from the book of Isaiah, that these people honor me with their lips, but their hearts are far from me (see Mark 7). In other words, why are you doing this tradition if it's not leading to inner change?

Traditions can get in the way of actually doing the will of God. You can do a lot of external rituals, but it may lead to zero internal effect.

The Pharisees were evaluating Jesus and his disciples based on their traditions and not God's will. Worst, their tradition was putting a distance between them and the very people they were meant to reach. The call of God on their lives was to reach the Gentiles, not keep away from them.

Their tradition became an obstacle. It became a prejudice against Gentiles. It created this divide between them and those outside of their tradition.

Jesus came to challenge all religious traditions. In a sense, Jesus says if a tradition is not motivating you to love God and people, it is an empty ritual. It should make us question, why are we doing this?

Traditions that have been ingrained in us for centuries are hard to break. It has a tight grip on us. We can keep doing them year after a year and not realizing that it's actually making us more miserable and away from God and the people we are meant to reach.

Depending on your religious upbringing, there are countless traditions that can become empty rituals. Things like how to pray, style of worship, what to eat or not eat, clothing that is appropriate or inappropriate, denomination dogmas, even Bible translations...all of it can make you feel empty and void. Deep down inside, we ask, why are we doing this?

Unfortunately, religious traditions have a tendency of making everything black or white, when in fact a lot of these things are a matter of personal preference.

Not everything is a matter of right or wrong.

Many things are a matter of personal choice, conviction, and conscience before God.

Personal preferences are not eternal doctrine.

Fighting over the styles of music for worship, the use of technology in church, and ministry approaches are all matters of preference.

If you like a certain tradition or style, you can do it without imposing it on others. As long it is leading you to love God and love people.

Sometimes, following Jesus will rub against personal preferences. At that point, we must ask, what's most important to me? Doing my thing or doing God's will?

Jesus is mostly concerned with our hearts being aligned with God's hearts than doing empty traditions.

"And then he added, "It is what comes from inside that defiles you. For from within, out of a person's heart, come evil thoughts, sexual immorality, theft, murder, adultery, greed, wickedness, deceit, lustful desires, envy, slander, pride, and foolishness. All these vile things come from within; they are what defile you."" - **Mark 7:20-23**

In other words, we can wash our hands all day long, but it won't cleanse our hearts.

The Pharisees didn't ask why Jesus' disciples don't follow God, but their own tradition.

Sometimes, religious people are more concerned with what looks good externally instead of what's causing internal transformation.

External rituals without internal transformation is useless.

Traditions are not the standard, Jesus is.

Traditions don't change people, Jesus does.

Only Jesus can change us from the inside out.

Jesus is an expert on the human heart. He goes straight to the heart. The real issue is in the heart of mankind. Jesus focuses on heart surgery that leads to real change. We don't need more empty rituals, but a heart transplant. We need Jesus to work on us from the inside out.

If you go to church, that's a good tradition, but why do you go to church?

You sang some songs at church, that's good, but did you mean what you sang? Did it truly connect you with God?

You pray, that's good, but did you actually pray to a loving God and felt connected to Him? Or was it just empty words?

You give offerings in church, that's good, but did you give it from a place of gratitude or out of obligation or manipulation?

You serve on a ministry team, that's good, but did you have a heart for people? Or was it just formality?

If our hearts are not attached, then these are just empty traditions.

Jesus is after our hearts, because he's after the real us.

So what's the point of any religious traditions if it's not leading us to love God and people more?

We now exchange gifts around 9pm on Christmas Eve and everyone is happy.

CHAPTER 5

JESUS VERSUS HIS FOLLOWERS

"Anyone who is not against us is for us." - ***Mark 9:40***

I HEARD THAT Ghandi was fascinated by Jesus. Especially, Jesus' Sermon on the Mount. Ghandi, a peaceful activist, found Jesus to be very inspirational. But, he had an issue with the people who professed to be followers of Jesus.

It is said that Ghandi, speaking to these so called followers of Jesus said, "I like your Christ, I do not like your Christians. Your Christians are so unlike your Christ."

Wow.

Why is there a disconnect between Jesus and his so called "followers" at times?

The original disciples of Jesus saw some people casting out demons in Jesus' name and they tried to stop them because these people were not a part of the "crew." But, Jesus told them not to stop them because if they are not against us, they are for us (see Mark 9).

I think it's possible to be sincere and wrong at the same time. So many have been sincere about doing the will of God, but wrong in their approach.

I like the way we do church. I believe in it. I think it's a great approach. But, that does not mean that other approaches to church are wrong.

Jesus compares Church with a body. He says we are His body.

There are 20 major arteries in the human body, which then branch of into several much smaller arterioles and capillaries. I googled it.

All of these veins and arteries are working together for the good of the same body.

It would be foolish and detrimental for these veins to stop each other from doing their valuable work within the body.

I see this Jesus movement as a beautiful and messy and mosaic and complex and diverse body of people from all walks of life, races and cultures, tribes and languages.

Actually it's what the Bible describes:

> "After this I saw a vast crowd, too great to count, from every nation and tribe and people and language, standing in front of the throne and before the Lamb. They were clothed in white robes and

held palm branches in their hands."
- ***Revelation 7:9***

There's a dangerous theology of who's in and who's out that's harmful to the Jesus movement.

The Bible seems to emphasize that God is seeking to reconcile the entire world to Himself.

Sometimes, I think we struggle to understand the difference between unity and uniformity. I don't have to look, dress, and talk like you to want the same things you want.

My kids go to a school where they have to wear a uniform, but that does not mean that every kid and teacher are united.

Different is not bad.

Some people's experience will be different than mine.

My wife, Lindsey, and I have very different experiences when it comes to church and following Jesus.

I had a radical encounter with Jesus at the age of 20 that shifted my entire life. I felt like scales were removed from my heart and eyes, and nothing has ever been the same since.

Lindsey grew up in a Christian home, where at a very young age, she invited Jesus into her life and gradually began to understand what that actually means.

When we met in college, I was a very zealous young dude who thought everyone needs to have the same experience as me. Me and her have an ongoing joke that I was a mini Pharisee. I still have to fight those zealous urges today.

No one owns the copyright on the Jesus movement.

That's why no vein or expression of this movement is better than the other. We are all part of the same body.

Jesus is inclusive, religion is exclusive.

> "Jesus told him, "I am the way, the truth, and the life. No one can come to the Father except through me."
> - ***John 14:6***

Jesus is the way and that is exclusive.

Anyone can follow Jesus, and that is inclusive.

Jesus is the only way to God, but all are welcome.

Our enemy is not a different vein from the same body.

Our physical body knows how to fight intruders, like germs and infections.

As followers of Jesus, we must learn to discern who is the real enemy to the body of Christ.

The church down the street from me is not the enemy.

If someone is preaching Jesus wrong, God will deal with them.

> "Those others do not have pure motives as they preach about Christ. They preach with selfish ambition, not sincerely, intending to make my chains more painful to me. But that doesn't matter. Whether their motives are false or genuine, the message about Christ is being preached either way, so I rejoice. And I will continue to rejoice."
> - **Philippians 1:17-18**

I love the Apostle Paul's attitude. Let them preach even if the motives are wrong. I don't have to play God.

For the first few years after Jesus lived, died, and rose again, what we know as Christianity today, was simply called "the way".

In the book of Acts, which follows the birth and expansion of this movement, we find that it's not until the gospel message reaches a city called Antioch, that the believers are called Christians.

Christians, as in like Christ.

It started as a mockery... "These people think they are like that Jesus person who calls Himself the Christ, or the Anointed One" (see Acts 11).

The name stuck. To be a Christian is to be like Jesus.

For centuries, this movement would continue to flourish and express itself in many veins of expression.

Fast forward to the 4th century, after years of intense persecution, Emperor Constantine made Christianity the official religion of Rome.

This affected the Jesus movement deeply.

On one side, it helped to minimize the persecution against those who believe in Jesus.

On the other hand, it was the beginning of the era of institutionalized Christianity.

This vein of the body became known as the Roman Catholic Church. Catholic means universal.

Again, we can be sincere and wrong.

The goal was to unify the church through the Roman Empire, but it led to the church being controlled by the Roman government, which led to a politically driven church.

The church was officially institutionalized.

But, there's always a group of people who don't conform, because they believe that the Jesus movement is bigger than any institution of government.

Many other veins of the body of Christ continued to push the gospel forward without being controlled by the Empire.

In the 16th century, many were frustrated with the state of the church under the Roman Empire. People were fed up with the politics and legalism.

A catholic priest, by the name of Martin Luther, began to read the Bible and found a disconnect between the church and the gospel of Jesus.

One particular verse in the book of Romans, struck a deep nerve within him:

> "This Good News tells us how God makes us right in his sight. This is accomplished from start to finish by faith. As the Scriptures say, "It

is through faith that a righteous person has life."" - **Romans 1:17**

Martin Luther was awakened to the reality that Jesus alone is our salvation and not indulgences and dogmas of the Church of Rome.

This began what we call the Protestant reformation of the church.

It split the body into two main veins.

The Catholic vein and the Protestant vein.

Which led to the birth of mainstream denominations as we know them today.

Martin felt compelled to translate the Bible into the language of the people. Up to this point, only the priests were allowed to read the Bible.

There is no right Christian denomination.

Denominations are born out of certain convictions within a person.

In other words, it's about which doctrines (teachings) in the Bible we value most.

Again, it's many veins within a body. No vein is more important than the other, and to fight over it is foolish. And it's missing the mark, which is another word for sinning.

I am part of a non-denomination tradition. Meaning, we are not a mainstream denomination like Baptist, Lutheran, Pentecostal, Methodist...

Funny thing is, being a non-denominational church is a denomination in itself.

The point is, this Jesus body has many veins.

We can celebrate them.

And learn from each other.

Some of my favorite writers, come from the Catholic vein: Henri Nouwen & Thomas Merton.

Some of my favorite songs are hymns from centuries ago. For example, "A Mighty Fortress is Our God" by Martin Luther.

Some of my favorite preachers come from different denominations like Charles Spurgeon, TD Jakes, Jentezen Franklin, and John Wesley.

I've done Catholic weddings, because I'm friends with a priest.

I grew up going to Sunday school at a Nazarene church in the morning and Catholic mass at night.

I had a personal encounter with Jesus in a Nazarene family camp.

I speak in tongues, and some of my friends don't speak in tongues, but we love Jesus.

Jesus has some strong language for people who have a hard time embracing the many veins of His body:

> ""But if you cause one of these little ones who trusts in me to fall into sin, it would be better for you to be thrown into the sea with a large millstone hung around your neck."
> - **Mark 9:42**

If someone is following Jesus in whatever vein of expression and we cause them to stop, we are coming up against Jesus Himself.

We must be careful to not allow our personal preferences get in the way of people following Jesus.

Without the many veins of the same body, we would get an incomplete picture of the body of Christ.

We all need a tribe to belong to. And that is why I think God loves the different veins of expression so everyone can find a place to call their home church.

And if they are not against us, they are for us.

United we stand.

One body.

Many veins.

CHAPTER 6

JESUS VERSUS SELF-RIGHTEOUSNESS

"Jesus looked at them intently and said, "Humanly speaking, it is impossible. But not with God. Everything is possible with God."" - **Mark 10:27**

"GOD DOES NOT like me." That's what my boss told me one day. I was in college and working one of the many odd jobs, as we all do when in college or when trying to figure out what to do with our lives.

I worked in this small family owned factory. We made electrical parts. The job was monotonous, but I liked it. The reason I liked this job is that I was still in the honeymoon phases of my spiritual awakening. This job gave me a chance to deepen my understanding of following Jesus. I would go to work, put on my walkman and listen to preaching tapes. Wait, I said Walkman. Remember those? For millennials out there, Walkman was the iPod of your elders.

I became friends with the factory owner and we would spend time talking about everything under the sun. One day, I decided to buy him a Bible. And he began reading it.

One morning he came in upset. He told me that as he was reading the gospels, he came across the story of Jesus and the rich young ruler.

In this story, this rich young ruler approached Jesus and asked him, what he must do to inherit eternal life? By the way, he started his question by addressing Jesus as a good teacher.

Eternal life in the Jewish context, was not about dying and going to heaven someday. For them eternal life had a much deeper meaning. It meant how to live life right now on this planet to the fullest. It meant how to have meaning, fulfillment and purpose on this earth.

Right here.

Right now.

Not some pie in the sky some day.

In a way, it's like asking, how do I bring heaven to earth now in my life.

It is so much more meaningful than the lame understanding of waiting to die and go to heaven.

Jesus as usual, gives this young ruler an interesting answer. Actually instead of an answer, he asks him a question. Typical Jesus.

Jesus is always looking to help us wrestle with something deeper within us.

What's the real question behind your question?

Why do you call me good?, Jesus asked him.

In other words, what are your standards of good(ness)?

In Jesus' teachings, his emphasis is always the difference between humanity's standards and God's standards.

In a way, humanity's standards seems to be outward focused, or external. What can be seen and measured.

God's standards go deeper than what we can see and measure. God's standards are internal - matters of the heart and soul.

We equate morality with doing good, not being good.

The rich young ruler seems to have a lot going for him.

Young, which many of us wish we still were.

Rich, meaning that he did not have any financial struggles to live a good life.

Ruler, meaning he had status in society.

Still, he comes to ask Jesus this most important question: how do I live a fulfilled life?

Why do you call me good? Jesus says. He's trying to elevate this young rulers thinking and perspective.

Jesus is not only a good moral teacher, He is God in the flesh.

It's like Jesus is saying to him, and to us... Are you looking for the human standard of good or are you looking for the source of goodness, who is God? Wow.

You are looking for God not good, but God is good.

A true relationship with God is what brings fulfillment, meaning, and purpose in life.

So eternal life is not about being good according to human standards.

Eternal life is being in right relationship with Jesus, who is God.

Jesus is saying, it's not good (morality) that you need; you need God.

What must I do? That question implies self-will.

If it's about what you can do, then it's about you, not God.

That's why Jesus tests him with the commandments. He thinks his moral good standing can give him eternal life.

Jesus chose to focus on the second part of the Ten Commandments; all of the ones relating to how to treat others.

The young ruler seems to nail all the external commandments.

But, do you love God above all else, including yourself?

You can think that you are good and moral, therefore, you have no need for God.

That is why the first commandment is about not having any other gods, including self.

And that is why Jesus checks his heart. He tells the young ruler to go sell everything and come back and follow Jesus into eternal life. The young ruler left the presence of Jesus, sad (see Mark 10).

What do you really value?

Do you love God above everything?

For the young ruler, money and possession was everything.

But, it's not one size fits all.

We all have little idols in our hearts that gets in the way of God.

For some, like Nicodemus who came to Jesus at night, its religious tradition.

For the Samaritan women, it was relationships and the fear of being lonely.

For Judas, his political views of the Messiah, made him betray Jesus.

For the record, there are many rich people in the Bible.

Money is a great resource, but a terrible god.

What is the thing or the person that keeps you from loving God with all your heart, mind, soul and strength?

Anything or anyone that we put above God becomes an hindrance to eternal life: meaning, fulfillment and purpose.

Nothing else or no one else will truly fulfill you.

The young rich ruler was sad when he walked away from Jesus. And Jesus was sad for him.

Jesus is sad that this young ruler walked away from what he needed most - a savior.

And that is why my boss was sad and angry by reading this encounter.

Eternal life from self-perspective is impossible.

Self-righteousness is when I get to decide how to be in good standing with God and others.

The thing with eternal life is that you can not earn it.

And you do not deserve it.

It is a gift from God to us.

> "Salvation is not a reward for the good things we have done, so none of us can boast about it. For we are God's masterpiece. He has created us anew in Christ Jesus, so we can do the good things he planned for us long ago." - **Ephesians 2:9-10**

I think there's a play on words in this encounter with the rich young ruler.

I think rich symbolizes self-sufficiency.

This idea that, I can manage without the grace of God. I've got my health, my family, my friends, my wealth, my status…but still my heart longs for meaning and purpose. It longs for God.

Jesus is always giving us these weird analogies to make his point.

> "In fact, it is easier for a camel to go through the eye of a needle than for a rich person to enter the Kingdom of God!"" - **Mark 10:25**

Sounds weird and bizarre.

But, this is Jesus' humor and sarcasm at its best. For those who have a hard time with associating Jesus with sarcasm, the word logic might be more appropriate.

Camels, were a mean of transportation in those days.

Each city had these gates that you had to get through to get into the city. And some of these gates were called needles.

Camels being tall animals had a hard time getting through those gates (needles).

The owners of these camels would have to struggle with them to get them through these gates.

It was a constant pull and tug for some time until the camel can submit himself into these gates. The owner must get the camel to bow his head in order to get through the needle.

The interesting thing is that the camel would be exhausted from these long journeys and does not realize that on the other side of the gate is food and water waiting for him.

And that's the irony of the eternal life that Jesus is offering to us.

We kick and scream because we hold on to all of these things we believe are so important, not realizing that on the other side of our submission, we will find God's provisions for our lives.

This is why the Bible says that God gives grace to the humble, but opposes the proud (see James 4).

That is why that young rich ruler and my boss were sad.

Jesus is our righteousness.

His blood and sacrifice on the cross cleanses us from all self-righteousness.

> "God has united you with Christ Jesus. For our benefit God made him to be wisdom itself. Christ made us right with God; he made us pure and holy, and he freed us from sin." - ***1 Corinthians 1:30***

This encounter between Jesus and the young rich ruler, reminds of what the great-late missionary Jim Elliot said:

"He is no fool who gives what he cannot keep to gain that which he cannot lose."

We cannot lose with Jesus.

CHAPTER 7

WHO IS JESUS?

Who do you say I am? - ***Jesus***

WILL THE REAL Slim Shady please stand up?

Remember that song?

That's when we were introduced to the Hip-Hop genius called Eminem.

There are many versions of Jesus.

It makes you want to ask, will the real Jesus please stand up?

Jesus himself asked the question, who do people say that I am?

At this time, Jesus had been doing his ministry for about three years. His popularity was growing as a teacher, healer, and prophet.

> ""Well," they replied, "some say John the Baptist, some say Elijah, and others say Jeremiah or one of the other prophets."" - **Matthew 16:14**

People had different opinions of Jesus. And that has not changed 2,000 years later.

Some see Jesus as a great moral teacher. Others see him as a prophet, revolutionary, radical leader.

Same Jesus, different opinions. Why?

Allow me to propose an equation to answer that question:

Proximity + Intimacy = Experience.

We all have a certain opinion of someone, but that opinion can change as you get closer to that person.

That's why I think, Jesus had to ask that question twice.

First, he asked, who do people say I am? And then followed up with who do you say I am?

The second question was directed to his first students. They had been together every single day for about three years. Because, when a rabbi, or teacher asked you to follow him, it meant literally being together every single day, 24/7, 365 days.

Jesus was saying, it's one thing for people to have a mere opinion of me based on limited exposure to who I really am, and it's another thing for you who have been with me everyday for the past three years.

The more we spend time knowing Jesus, the greater the revelation of who he truly is.

This is deeper than mere opinion.

Deeper than just going to church services.

Deeper than just doing religious activities.

The more we spend time with Jesus, the greater the experience.

> "Simon Peter said, "You're the Christ, the Messiah, the Son of the living God."" - ***Matthew 16:16***

Like Peter, we all need a divine revelation of Jesus.

A divine encounter with Him.

When we were in school, we often wondered if what we are learning would actually be useful in the real world.

For me, it was math. What's the point of algebra and Calculus?

God could not have possibly invented math! He's not a God of confusion.

Who do you say Jesus is, is the ultimate question in life.

This is not merely a question of knowledge and information that will never affect the real world.

This question has implications for how I live.

It is a question that can profoundly affect my worldview.

It affects my convictions and lifestyle.

How I answer that question, impacts the other deep questions I have in life:

Who am I?

Why am I here?

Where am I going?

> For in him we live and move and
> have our being. - **Acts 17:28**

If Jesus is the Christ, the anointed one, God in the flesh, then it deeply affects my existence as a human being.

Jesus is fully human and fully divine.

100% man and 100% God.

If you lean on one side or the other, you will not get the Jesus of the Bible.

Some stumble over his humanity and others stumble over his divinity.

It's a great mystery.

> "Jesus replied, "You are blessed, Simon son of John, because my Father in heaven has revealed this to you. You did not learn this from any human being." - **Matthew 16:17**

According to Jesus, God the Father has to reveal that to us about Him.

It is a divine experience to know Jesus in this capacity.

Revelation, means to unveil or uncover. It is God's disclosure of Himself.

Jesus was fully human.

He was born from a woman.

He had to grow physically, emotionally, and spiritually.

He ate food, got tired, and frustrated at times.

He had real emotions, friends and enemies.

He cried, he felt lonely, he laughed and was comical.

He felt pain, betrayal, and he worked with his hands.

He was an amazing storyteller.

He lived a fully human life, for about 33 years.

Jesus was fully divine.

He didn't have an earthly father, for He was conceived by the Holy Spirit.

At the age of 12, He said he must be about His heavenly father's business on earth.

He performed many miracles.

Demons were afraid of him and they acknowledge him as God's son.

He walked on water.

He brought people back from the dead.

He laid hands on the sick and healed them.

He forgave sins.

He called Himself, I Am. What God called Himself in the Old Testament.

He fulfilled over 300 prophecies during his lifetime.

When I was 20 years old, my life was forever changed by Jesus.

I always believed in God, but now I had a divine revelation from God.

Jesus changed my entire worldview.

I heard a voice say that I was living in vain. It broke me. I was sobbing like a baby. At the same time, I felt loved and approved. Again, a great mystery, but that's how Jesus works through His Spirit.

A few months later, I had a second revelation that I was meant to preach the gospel.

Since then, Jesus has set me free from destructive patterns.

He has healed me and continues to heal me physically, emotionally and spiritually.

He put a passion in me for preaching and helping people connect with him.

He led to me to meet my wife, Lindsey.

He led us to plant a church in New Bedford, MA.

He leads me everyday.

Jesus molds me as a man, husband, father, friend and pastor.

There's not an area in my life that Jesus has not influenced.

Who am I? - I am a child of God

Why am I here? - To know God and make Him known.

Where am I going? - To live with Jesus for all eternity.

Who do you say Jesus is?

Ask Him for a divine revelation.

CHAPTER 8

FRIEND

"There is no greater love than to lay down one's life for one's friends." - **John 15:13**

A GOOD FRIEND is rare commodity.

Remember the kindergarten threats? "I'm not your friend anymore!" Those words cut deep.

Friendship is a universal craving.

I think the ultimate test of a great friendship is if I can visit your house and open your fridge.

Jesus changes the game on the teacher and student relationship.

> "I no longer call you slaves, because a master doesn't confide in his slaves. Now you are my friends, since I have told you everything the Father told me." - **John 15:15**

No longer just a rabbi, teacher to student relationship. But, a friendship.

I was a high school teacher for nine years and a Bible ministry teacher for four years.

In order to maintain professionalism and accountability, we try not to get too close to the students. It is healthy for both the teacher and students.

Jesus is not afraid to get close to us.

I think it's one of the things that separates Jesus from mere religions.

Jesus calls his followers his friends.

God is not a taskmaster, but a friend.

Friendship is much deeper and personal than just following some dogmas and religious requirements.

> "The difference between a servant and a friend is not between diligent obedience and disobedience (or even casual obedience). The difference is between understanding and not understanding. Because friends have a close relationship, they understand while servants do not." - **David Guzik**

Jesus says that we are his friend if we do what he commanded. Basically to love one another as He loved us.

Friends understand the blessings of obedience.

A major key to any healthy friendship is harmony through obedience. A mutual desire to honor one another.

Because of the messiness of religion, most people don't view Jesus as a friend.

They have been taught a sterile Jesus that only wants you to maintain certain moral standards and check certain religious boxes.

Which leads to a cold and distant God who demands obedience without relationship.

"God's grace invites you - no, requires you - to change your attitude about yourself and take sides with God against feelings of rejection." - Max Lucado

Jesus displays God-friend.

A friend through the good, the bad and the ugly of life.

friend

A friend who sticks closer than a brother:

…when you are struggling to pay your bills.

…when tragedy hits.

…when you go to the mall (find a sale).

…when you fall in love.

…when your heart is broken.

Small things, trivial things, and big things.

A friend who proves His love by giving His life.

I enjoy spending time with Jesus.

His presence is so tangible at times.

I can talk with Jesus about everything.

Nothing is too big or too small.

Just like when you can talk to a friend.

Way before Jesus came to earth, a prophet named Isaiah, said this about Jesus:

> "For a child is born to us, a son is given to us. The government will rest on his shoulders. And he will be called: Wonderful Counselor, Mighty God, Everlasting Father, Prince of Peace." - ***Isaiah 9:6***

Jesus is a counselor when you need one.

A mighty God when you need Him to be.

A Father for all times.

Peace in the midst of chaos.

Religious taskmasters only bark out orders.

They don't let you in on their plans and purpose.

Jesus wants you to know the will of the Father.

He plans to prosper you, to give you hope and a future, as the prophet Jeremiah tells us.

I told you, I love old hymns.

One of my favorites is what a friend we have in Jesus:

What a friend we have in Jesus

All our sins and griefs to bear

And what a privilege to carry

Everything to God in prayer

Oh, what peace we often forfeit

Oh, what needless pain we bear

All because we do not carry

Everything to God in prayer.

We can be friends with Jesus through His Spirit.

And His Spirit empowers us to live in obedience and harmony with Him.

Jesus fills us with your Spirit that we may live in this divine friendship with you.

CHAPTER 9

LOVED & APPROVED

"And a voice came out of heaven saying: "You are My beloved Son, in You I am well-pleased and delighted!"" - **Mark 1:11**

I AM FASCINATED by Jesus.

It's been over 2000 years since he walked the earth, but we are still experiencing his power, love and impact.

Even if you don't believe in him as the son of God, you must admit that he's very intriguing.

Why is Jesus still so relevant today?

As I write this, I'm thinking about the people who recently got baptized at our church. Each one of them shared a unique experience of how Jesus has changed their lives. It is fascinating to me that even though some of these people don't know each other and have different upbringings and life experiences, they all say that this Jesus has made a tangible difference in their lives. Amazing!

When you read the gospels, you come across the fact that Jesus got baptized. And it makes you question, why?

If Jesus is the son of God, which implies that he's equal with God, then he does not have a sinful past that he needs to repent from. So why?

One of the things that all of us struggle to understand is the fact that Jesus was fully human. He was 100% man.

> "Though he was God, he did not think of equality with God as something to cling to. Instead, he gave

up his divine privileges; he took the humble position of a slave and was born as a human being. When he appeared in human form," - **Philippians 2:6-7**

Jesus fully surrenders himself to the human experience in order to point us back to God, the Father.

Jesus grew up in a small village. Everyone knew everyone. And not everyone believed that Mary was a virgin who got pregnant by God's Spirit. Would you believe her?

So imagine growing up in this small village and hearing rumors about how you were conceived?

Jesus had to grow up with this stigma in the back of his mind. Especially in that time period that having a baby out of wedlock was a major sin. What do you think that does to someone's psyche?

Jesus knowing who he truly was and is, chooses to embrace the full human experience, which includes being treated with contempt at times.

When we get to his baptism, Jesus is about 30 years old. We don't know much about his life between the ages of 12-30yrs. He basically lived in obscurity for about 18 years of his life. Waiting for God's timing to go public with his earthly ministry.

He embraces baptism to fully submit to the Father's plan of redemption. This moment symbolizes Jesus' coming out party. It's time to go public with God's eternal plan.

And in this moment, the Father validates Jesus as his son.

> "And a voice from heaven said, "You are my dearly loved Son, and you bring me great joy."" - **Mark 1:11**

We all crave validation from our parents.

We want them to be proud of us.

As a parent of five kids, I'm constantly hearing my kids say, "daddy look what I can do! Did you see that?"

We are all hungry for validation and approval.

We crave love and acceptance.

And most of us unfortunately carry around father wounds from lack of validation.

God the Father knows that Jesus being fully human was no different. Waiting in obscurity and being exposed to much contempt, Jesus needed to be validated by his Father.

So Jesus' baptism is the Father speaking to all of us.

You are loved.

I am pleased with you.

Says God the Father.

Australian activist and preacher Christine Caine puts it this way:

"Your life is just a process of learning who you truly are."

Before Jesus goes public with his ministry to the world, the Father says, you are already approved by me.

Jesus' validation does not come from what he can do for the Father. He will preach, perform miracles, gather crowds, but those acts will not define him.

Who we are determines what we do.

We are human beings, not human doings.

We are loved and approved by our Heavenly Father.

To be a follower of Jesus is to live in Jesus. Meaning, we live in the reality of who Jesus is and what he has done on our behalf.

We embrace his baptism as our baptism. So when we get baptized we embrace the words of the Father over our own lives. We are loved and approved.

In Jesus' death, we are forgiven, we are justified and we are accepted.

> "So now there is no condemnation for those who belong to Christ Jesus." - **Romans 8:1**

This is the grace of God over us.

We never graduate from the grace of God.

We continue to grow in his grace and truth.

Everything that we do must first flow from this place of grace.

God's grace gives us our true identity.

True fulfillment will only come from knowing who we are in Jesus.

When we embrace Jesus, we forsake our old identity and embrace who we truly are in Him.

> "This means that anyone who belongs to Christ has become a new person. The old life is gone; a new life has begun!" - ***2 Corinthians 5:17***

At our church, we like to call this the new normal. Which by the way, we had been saying this way before COVID-19. As I'm writing this we are still in the middle of this pandemic and are living the new normal.

But, for us as followers of Jesus, the new normal began the day we embrace Jesus as our Leader and Savior.

In Jesus we feel loved and approved.

We are God's children, redeemed by the blood of Jesus on the cross.

When Jesus rose from the grave three days later, we also rose with him to a new life.

This new life is filled with God's love and approval. Therefore, we live from a place of acceptance. We are not trying to earn God's love or anyone's approval. We know we don't earn nor do we deserve it, because it is a gift from God to us.

When you untangle Jesus from all the religious hoops, you end up with his grace, which is an unmerited gift.

CHAPTER 10

A NEW COMMANDMENT

> "So now I am giving you a new commandment: Love each other. Just as I have loved you, you should love each other." - ***John 13:34***

SO FAR, WE have tried to untangle Jesus from legalism, traditions, personal preferences and self-righteousness. I hope that it's helping to clear the way for us to see Jesus in a new light.

As Jesus' life on earth was coming to an end, he had a pivotal time with his close disciples. He has a dinner with them. Once again, we see the relational heart of Jesus towards those he loves.

He eats with them. You share meals with those that you love and want to cultivate a close connection.

In this particular meal, Jesus did something completely new and revolutionary.

As Jewish people, the disciples were used to having the Passover meal to celebrate and remember their history as God's people. They would retell their story from the days of slavery under the Egyptians and how God came to deliver them through the leadership of Moses.

The Passover meal had been a part of their tradition for many centuries, but here Jesus changes its meaning forever.

"Remember me." Jesus says.

Do this in my memory.

Jesus takes a couple of typical staples of their custom meal and connects them to himself and to what he's about to do.

Instead of them remembering what happened in Egypt, Jesus says remember what I am about to do.

Jesus says that the bread will now symbolize his broken body on the cross. And the wine is blood spilled for the forgiveness of sin.

This is the new exodus. Or better yet, a new entrance into a deeper communion with God.

In Jesus, the world is about to be fully reconciled to God. This sacrifice is not just for a group of people, but for everyone, everywhere.

Jesus tells them that through a new commandment, the world will know that they follow Him.

> "Your love for one another will prove
> to the world that you are my disci-
> ples."" - ***John 13:35***

This is mind blowing for me.

Jesus meets with his close disciples, has a meal with them, in which he reveals what he's about to do on the cross and tells them by loving one another, the world will know that they are his disciples.

And that has changed the world and still is changing the world.

Jesus' selfless sacrifice on the cross changed the world forever.

But, his disciples needed to carry his message forward with a new commandment of loving one another.

In a natural sense, the Jesus movement should not have made it this far. It should have died down within a few years. There are many religious teachers who claim to want to change the world, but their movements don't last long.

The Jesus movement began in a very obscure part of the world. A place that was considered to be a ghetto under the Roman Empire. A place of extreme poverty and limited freedom.

Why did the Jesus movement grow?

Something supernatural took place on that weekend over 2000 years ago.

The meal, the cross, and the resurrection changed the world forever.

Since then, our calendar has been split between B.C and A.D, all because of Jesus.

Jesus split history into two eras.

Before and after Jesus.

Whether someone believes or not that Jesus is the savior of the world, that's hard to ignore.

Better still, it's hard to ignore his followers who are truly known by Jesus' new commandment of loving one another. That's what made his move-ment so powerful and still ongoing.

After the resurrection of Jesus, his followers were filled with His Spirit and began to spread the good news.

What they believed was not necessarily new. In those days, people believed in many gods and approaches to life. And people were not very impressed with new teachings. They would look at you with much skepticism. Almost like living in New England in the 21st century. We live in a very cynical place and people are not quick to buy what you are selling. This is New England baby.

The first disciples or believers did not have the New Testament Bible.

They did not have church buildings.

They did not have websites and social media.

All they had was the reality of that last meal, Jesus' death on the cross, his resurrection, and His Spirit in them.

And that was enough and it still is enough.

They set out to live his new commandment.

Love one another as I have love you, Jesus said.

How did Jesus love?

> "But God showed his great love
> for us by sending Christ to die
> for us while we were still sinners."
> - ***Romans 5:8***

There's nothing cute or soft about his love.

It is sacrificial love.

They set out to love the same way.

And that's what made Jesus' movement so com-pelling and attractive.

It wasn't so much what they were teaching from a religious standpoint, but how they lived and loved people, because of their personal experi-ence with Jesus.

They gained people's trust by their tangible love.

They valued everyone, regardless of race, gender, and social status.

They helped those in need. They reached the out-casts of society. They welcomed the unwelcome. They resisted the oppositions by loving them.

It is very hard to resist those who love you with no strings attached.

These first believers embodied the good news of Jesus.

They became the church of Jesus.

Church: a group of people that makes you feel like God has not given up on the world.

Jesus is right in the midst of them.

The church, God's people who seek to live out Jesus' new commandment, are the reason why this movement continues to grow all over the world.

I hear stories of followers of Jesus in Iran who are living this out in very difficult situations.

In China, they have to meet underground, because their government is opposed to this movement. But, still they find a way to meet and spread the good news.

When you untangle Jesus from all of the religious dogmas and unnecessary trappings, you are left with the reality of a meal, a cross, a resurrection, His Spirit, and His people called the Church.

Jesus' followers are now a reflection of Jesus on this earth.

To be a Christian is to be a mini-Christ.

Followers of Jesus are compelled to ask daily, what does love require of me?

And by Jesus' Spirit we look to demonstrate that love in tangible ways.

It's more than a dogma or set of rules and regulations.

It is a way of life.

It is the Jesus way of life.

CHAPTER 11

EVERYDAY LOVE

Who is my neighbor? - *Luke 10:29*

JESUS SAID THAT his followers will be known by the way they love one another.

It is how the world will know that we are actually followers of Jesus.

So what does love require of me?

Most us are familiar with the concept of the Good Samaritan.

Few of us actually understand the original setting of that story.

An expert in Mosaic Law had asked Jesus the question about eternal life. Remember, that question? How do I live a meaningful and purposeful life.

Jesus as always tests the motive of the question.

This expert seem to be more interested in testing Jesus, instead of being completely genuine.

> "Jesus replied, "What does the law of Moses say? How do you read it?" The man answered, "'You must love the Lord your God with all your heart, all your soul, all your strength, and all your mind.' And, 'Love your neighbor as yourself.'" "Right!" Jesus told him. "Do this and you will live!" The man wanted to justify his actions, so he asked Jesus, "And who is my neighbor?""
> - **Luke 10:26-29**

This is the issue of religion minus the heart of God.

It leads to again self-righteousness and head knowledge, instead of a heart filled with love that leads to action.

Since he was only concerned with justifying himself, Jesus tells him the story of the Good Samaritan.

In order to fully appreciate this story and it's implication, you must be a bit familiar with the context. It is a very provocative story.

Jewish and Samaritans did not get along.

This rift dates back to many centuries. Since the split of Israel into two kingdoms.

The Northern kingdom began mingling with a foreign nation called the Assyrians, and their illicit relationships gave birth to the Samaritans.

For the Southern kingdom Jew, the Samaritans were less than humans. They called them half-breeds and dogs.

Since then, they had developed two completely separate ways of life, including their approach to God. They each had their own version of Judaism and their own separate places of worship.

So when this Jewish scholar asked Jesus who is my neighbor, Jesus replies with the story where the Samaritan is actually the hero. Someone whom this Jewish man saw as a half-breed. Shots fired. Bang, bang Jesus.

It is like a member of the KKK asking Jesus who is my neighbor and he replies a black person.

Or a member of the bloods gang asking the same question and Jesus replies with a crip member.

Religion without the heart of Jesus divides people into categories.

In this story, a man has been robbed, beaten and left by the side of the road.

A priest walking by sees him lying there and walks the other way.

A levite (worship leader) also passes by the man and walks the other way.

These people were supposed to represent God. But, their hearts were not filled with the same love for people. Their religion actually keeps them from helping this man.

A Samaritan, who was despised by these religious people actually stops and helps this man. This Samaritan had enough compassion to stop and help.

> ""Now which of these three would you say was a neighbor to the man who was attacked by bandits?" Jesus asked. The man replied, "The one who showed him mercy." Then Jesus said, "Yes, now go and do the same."" - **Luke 10:36-37**

What does love require of me?

This is the question that has driven this Jesus movement forward for more than 2000 years.

Untangling Jesus from religion will lead us to everyday L.O.V.E for our neighbors, who is anyone we come in contact with.

So how do we **L.O.V.E** people in tangible ways?

First, we learn to **listen.**

A major component of love is simply listening. And somewhere my wife said Amen.

> "Understand this, my dear brothers and sisters: You must all be quick to listen, slow to speak, and slow to get angry." - **James 1:19**

The world needs better listeners.

A major part of praying is learning to listen to the voice of God.

The more we learn to be still and listen to God, the more we will be in tune with the needs of others around us, starting right at home.

Some days the most powerful thing we can do for others, is to simply be available to listen.

Second, we must learn to **obey** the promptings of Jesus' Spirit in us.

> "But don't just listen to God's word.
> You must do what it says. Otherwise,
> you are only fooling yourselves."
> - ***James 1:22***

As we walk with Jesus, His Spirit will nudge us towards the need of others.

Don't ignore His still small voice.

He might be speaking to you right now.

Pay attention to when he drops a name in your heart. Spring to action and reach out.

Obeying the promptings of God's Spirit is where the action is. It's where this Jesus becomes very real in tangible ways.

Third, we **value** every person tangibly.

When it comes to loving people like Jesus, the thought does not count. It's about action.

> "What good is it, dear brothers and sisters, if you say you have faith but don't show it by your actions? Can that kind of faith save anyone? Suppose you see a brother or sister who has no food or clothing, and you say, "Good-bye and have a good day; stay warm and eat well"— but then you don't give that person any food or clothing. What good does that do?" - **James 2:14-16**

According to Gary Chapman, we humans have five love languages:

1. Acts of service
2. Physical touch
3. Words of affirmation
4. Gifts
5. Quality time

To love like Jesus is to learn to speak others love language.

At home with our spouses and kids.

At our jobs, learning our co-workers love language.

In our communities, seeing people through their needs.

Don't assume that someone is all set.

Encourage someone out loud.

Just do it.

Fourth, we **empower** others to succeed.

Love believes in the potential of others.

> "Don't speak evil against each other, dear brothers and sisters. If you criticize and judge each other, then you are criticizing and judging God's law. But your job is to obey the law, not to judge whether it applies to you. God alone, who gave the law, is the Judge. He alone has the power to save or to destroy. So what right do you have to judge your neighbor?" - **James 4:11-12**

We love others by helping them take their next steps to success in life.

One of my favorite things to do for others is buying them books. I believe that in life we must constantly be learning something new. The word disciple means student. Jesus calls us to be students of life. When I give someone a book, I am empowering them to think and learn. The more our minds are open to new ideas, the more we tap into our God-given potential.

How can you help someone take their next step in life?

Following Jesus is about progressive revelation. Meaning that we are constantly evolving towards the person that God created us to become.

All of us can play a role in empowering others on their journey.

If you are a mom, help a new mom, because you know how overwhelming being a mother can be.

If you own a business, mentor a new business owner. Show them the ropes and help them avoid the pit falls.

As a follower of Jesus, don't settle for going to church, take an interest in someone who's just starting their spiritual journey and teach them to become a mature believer.

I hope you embrace the **L.O.V.E** challenge daily.

Go a step further and invite another person to get on this journey with you. You can ask each other daily, how did you **L.O.V.E** someone today?

HERE'S A 21 DAY CHALLENGE.

EACH DAY OF the week you will try to reflect *L.O.V.E: Listen. Obey. Value. Empower*

Monday: Listen

Read these verses and be still to listen to God's voice:

Week 1 - James 1:19

Week 2 - Psalm 23

Week 3 - Psalm 46

Tuesday: Obey

Meditate on these verses and ask the Spirit to show you how to obey throughout the day

Week 1 - John 5:19

Week 2 - Matthew 7:24

Week 3 - James 4:17

Wednesday: Value

Bless someone with an act of kindness

Week 1 - text someone

Week 2 - call someone

Week 3 - spend quality time with someone

Thursday: Empower

Ask someone, how can I help you?

Week 1 - family/friends

Week 2 - co-worker/classmate

Week 3 - stranger/neighbor

Friday: Action

Be a blessing in tangible ways to a non-profit place near you.

Week 1 - donate canned goods

Week 2 - donate bag of potatoes/rice

Week 3 - volunteer at a local non-profit

NOTES

Intro

Religions in the world. see https://www.reference.com/world-view/many-religions-world-8f3af083e8592895

Chapter 3

The Pharisees and the mosaic law. https://www.pursuegod.org/rules-pharisees/

Chapter 5

Ghandi quote: https://www.goodreads.com/quotes/22155-i-like-your-christ-i-do-not-like-your-christians

Chapter 6

Jim Elliot quote. https://www.goodreads.com/author/quotes/2125255.Jim_Elliot

Chapter 8

David Guzik quote. https://www.blueletterbible.org/Comm/guzik_david/StudyGuide2017-Jhn/Jhn-15.cfm?a=1012001

Max Lucado quote. https://maxlucado.com

What a friend we have in Jesus lyrics. https://library.timelesstruths.org/music/What_a_Friend_We_Have_in_Jesus/

Chapter 9

Christine Caine quote. Her instagram/
ChristineCaine

Chapter 11

Gary Chapman: five love languages. <u>https://</u>
<u>www.5lovelanguages.com/5-love-languages/</u>

CPSIA information can be obtained
at www.ICGtesting.com
Printed in the USA
BVHW072352020321
601492BV00007B/669